AN ANALYSIS OF CHANAKYA'S CONCEPT OF STATE AND ITS RELEVANCE TO THE CONTEMPORARY INDIA

VOLUME 2, ISSUE 3 OF BRILLOPEDIA

AASTHA SINHA | KASHISH DARAK AND VAISHNAVI N

Contents

Preface

"Start writing, no matter what. The water does not flow until the faucet is turned on".

• Louis L'Amour

Hundreds of students and professors are contributing their work to Brillopedia, we are here to provide ample information about Law and Contemporary issues. Our aim is to provide a platform for today's generation to express their views and ideas on law and contemporary law.

Publication

This research paper is published in volume 2, issue 3 of Brillopedia

CHAPTER ONE

ABSTRACT

Kautilya, popularly known as Chanakya, born in 3rd century BCE had a unique, ambiguous, multifaceted and an egocentric personality. He was known for his wisdom, courage and eccentricity. His lifelong work, Arthashastra is considered as science of politics. Picking the literal meaning, Arthashastra means 'scripture of wealth'. Chanakya gives a various theories and concepts in his writings of Arthashastra and ChanakyaNiti. He talks about topics related to kingdom, economy, foreign policy, general and many more. He gave some unusual suggestions. The Arthashastra was collected after examine numerous works on statecraft by other masters and many different Dharmashastras to ameliorate the performance or efficacy of the state and to study measures and strategies of run the state.[1]He saw 'decline' and 'progress' in a different light. Chanakya's political idea on state rotate on the Idea of kingship and it was repeated in the Indian subcontinent as he was in strong support of monarchy and he says monarchy can only lead to justice, happiness, just form of society and end of Matsanyaya. Arthashastra actually talks about protection and acquisition or governance of a territory. This gives the concept of well-organized territory. His Saptanga theory states the seven elements of state [territory]. They assist in the running of state for the improvement of the subjects and conduct Peace and Justice. In today's scenario the elements and of state as well as the prime definition of state itself has changed. This paper deals with relevance of his concept of state or elements of state to the contemporary Indian state. Kautilya's Arthashastra provides for various strategies for ideal governance.

Keywords: Arthashastra, Saptanga theory, territory, elements of state

[1]Gora ,Kautilya'sSaptanga Theory of State, aspirant forum, 2021
https://aspirantforum.com/2014/10/21/kautilyas-theory-of-the-state/

CHAPTER TWO

INTRODUCTION

Arthashastra, the masterwork of Kautilya is considered as one of the greatest books with immense historical significance. Arthashastra can be considered written as Kautilya instructing and guiding Chandragupta Maurya. The concepts construed are mostly derived from older texts and scripts. Kautilya also famously known as Chanakya primarily focuses on political realism in respect to the structure of state.[1]Kautilya describes 'Rajya' as the central theme. Monarchy was the type of government that prevailed during his time and the structure of state explained in Arthashastra is according to the system that existed during that period. His work contemplates the political and social systems of the 4th century B. C. and deals with practical government administration. As stated earlier Chanakya's ideas are not original but adapted from the predecessors to systemize and clarify the ideas of origin of the concept that is called as state in the contemporary times. [2]

Kautilya in his work mentions seven elements that comprise the state which are comprised by natural constituents while the present scenario consists of four elements namely population, territory, government and sovereignty. He writes that for effective working of any organization or state, efficient administration is the most important factor. He was clearly not interested in how the state was but with the process of building it into a mighty and vigorous one which is all prepared to face internal as well as external dangers. In respect to the perception of Chanakya, state is not merely any group or association which has a common purpose but one that works because of mutual action of each and every individual who is a part of the state. He also propounds all the aspects of society including its protective duty.[3]

According to Kautilya, the principle of Dharma is most essential for the existence of the state. Ancient India's sovereignty was neither monistic nor pluralistic but determined as pluralistically monism and was regarded as a source of integration and synthesis. The scope of Arthashastra is humongous.

[1]ShahabShabbier, Kautilya on Leadership: Lessons from Arthashastra, 2012

https://www.researchgate.net/publication/
230787420_Kautilya_on_Leadership_Lessons_from_Arthashastra

[2]Dr.TyagiRuchi, Theory of State in Kautilya'sArthashastra

https://msbrijuniversity.ac.in/assets/uploads/newsupdate/
Theory%20of%20State%20in%20Kautilya.pdf

[3]Prof.ChakrabortiTridib, Contemporary Relevance Of Kautilya's Theory And Diplomacy, 2016

https://www.academia.edu/32142310/
KAUTILYA_ARTICLE_PDF_pdf?email_work_card=view-paper

CHAPTER THREE

RESEARCH PROBLEM

The concept of state is neither defined in early or later Vedic literature nor in the Dharmashastras and dharma sutras which talk about the law of that period. It is considered that at the very first the state was defined by Kautilya in Arthashastra. He characterized state by an organic unity. According to Kautilya the royal command enforced by sanctions was considered as a law. The origin and merge of Danda into law was conceptualized as sovereignty. [1]He had an Austinian viewpoint. The seven elements guide the courses of all human relationships and is an important factor to maintain unity and solidarity. Kautilya states about the elements of state but the question itself arising that whether he defines state. The state in modern day scenario comprises of territory, population, government and most importantly sovereignty. The concept of sovereignty according to the Arthashastra is seen as king being the principle dharma, which varies from the current state. Sovereignty in ancient India was pluralistically monism. The elements and structure given by Kautilya gives a fair justification to governing of a territory which is falsely considered as him defining state.

RESEARCH QUESTIONS

- Does Kautilya'sArthashastra define state?
- Are the 'elements of Rajya' explained in Arthashastra relevant to the contemporary concept of state?

SCOPE AND LIMITATION

The research paper is initiated to understand the elements of state given by Chanakya in Arthashastra. The scope of the research paper is to find if Arthashastra defines state and relativity of its elements to contemporary India. The paper is centered to concept of state according to Chanakya and its relevance in contemporary India.

RESEARCH OBJECTIVES

- To understand Kautilya's interpretation of the structure of state.
- To analyze if the elements stated by Kautilya relevant to the contemporary Indian state.

HYPOTHESIS

The concepts explained in Kautilya'sArthashastra were primarily according to the period in which he prevailed. The constituents of state elucidated by Kautilya cannot be misinterpreted as the definition of a state.

METHODOLOGY

A doctrinal research methodology is validated for this research paper which includes sources collected from secondary sources such as journals, books, research papers and articles. These sources assist the researchers throughout the research project to have an analytical understanding of the topic, mark hypotheses and draw conclusions. The study of this research paper is descriptive and analytical.

[1]Gora , Kautilya'sSaptanga Theory of State, aspirant forum, 2021 https://aspirantforum.com/2014/10/21/kautilyas-theory-of-the-state/

CHAPTER FOUR

KAUTILYA'S INTERPRETATION OF THE STRUCTURE OF STATE

The Arthashastra is a compendium of various concepts such as economy, politics, civil services, regulations, organizations and departments, law and justice, foreign policy, defense and war and so on. The picture of the ideal Kautilyan state is comprised of well-organized, prosperous and state with bustling activity which may be a lot different from the reality. The idealism of Chanakya though adapted in various societies even now, it is also true that the application and practice of that idealism is quite different to what he described it as. Through Arthashastra, which is also called as an art and science of politics and diplomacy, Kautilya gives an overview of how ancient India was and explains the systemization and uniformity of law throughout the empire[1] that includes all the territories and wholly called as 'Rajya'.

Chanakya mainly focuses on two factors to maintain the balance between the people's welfare and state's resources and that is proper maintenance of law and order and an adequate administrative system. 'Artha', the word that has several meanings is closely connected with the concept of economy and material well-being, which is one of the important, factors the prosperity of any nation or state. He doesn't explicitly lay down the theory of social contract even though his views are similar to it nor does he mention any contracts to make the king all powerful. [2]

Kautilya describes that state which he narrates as Rajya is an organic entity. The basis for the same is the seven elements which he depicts as Saptanga which is essential for the harmony and constituent of the state. He explains that the state has a role of being a social reformer and represents it as the principle of unity and solidarity.

Furthermore, he narrates about the janapadas which are the small kingdoms and mahajanapadas which are more powerful and evolved version of janapadas in his work and this great transition marks the start of urban based culture and permanent settlement. He mainly emphasizes on the kingship which is one of the main elements of the Rajya in his period. According to him the king was expected to ensure both individual and social order instead of only focusing on punishing his subjects. He was authorized to work for the entire welfare of the state and that he should follow the 'Rajaniti' unquestionably.

Security and peace which are two of the most important needs, led the citizens of his time to follow Manu as their king in reference to the system of kingship. Chanakya also quotes the remarkable concept of Raja dharma with reference to the Mahabharata and asserts that it is important for the ruler to follow the same as he is the one who represents the interest of the society and deemed as the symbol of principle of dharma[3]. Through Arthashastra, Kautilya broke the tradition of minimal intervention of the state in law and justice and upheld the power of state to make laws on its own.

The idea of a state as an organic entity marks its emergence from the Greek-city states and the same concept was conventionally followed by the upcoming generations. According to Chanakya none of the territories should be titled as kingdom (state) unless it filled by people and controlled by the mass of power with the absolute authority over that territory. In a sense, Arthashastra does not actually concern itself with the question and concept of origin of state rather its central theme comprises of addressing the king, the single ruler of the Rajya or kingdom. It is stated that in his period, mostly the sovereign power lied with the king or the ruler whereas in the contemporary times it lies with the people in general.

Precisely, in his sphere of ideas, it is mentioned that the structure of state cannot be completely depicted as evil and thus providing it with the coercive power is no harm. To encapsulate, Kautilya provides an overall view of that state and its structure rather than independently defining it as an entity or a definite subject. In his vision, state is an aspect which is a part of social life and social organization.

[1]Prof.ChakrabortiTridib, Contemporary Relevance Of Kautilya's Theory And Diplomacy, 2016

[2]Prof. ChakrabortiTridib, Contemporary Relevance Of Kautilya's Theory And Diplomacy, 2016

https://www.academia.edu/32142310/ KAUTILYA_ARTICLE_PDF_pdf?email_work_card=view-paper

[3]Prof. ChakrabortiTridib, Contemporary Relevance Of Kautilya's Theory And Diplomacy, 2016

https://www.academia.edu/32142310/ KAUTILYA_ARTICLE_PDF_pdf?email_work_card=view-paper

CHAPTER FIVE

RELEVANCE OF CHANAKYA'S STATE ELEMENTS TO CONTEMPORARY INDIAN STATE

Chanakya's philosophy gives voice to state as central theme.He had talked over state's origin, nature and working. In concerning to origin of state he accepted the theory of social-cohesion.The development of the state through different stages is not discussed by ancient Indian writers. Kautilya narrates a well-organized state: Kingship, practical politics principles, the qualities of an ideal ruler should execute and according to Chanakyastate which is human institution should be operated by a human being only.Primarily, a political thought should be concerned with the definite territory and its functions.

Kautilya mentions about the seven elements of the state. He states the importance of each element in organizing and regulating the state, in 'Saptanga Theory'. They are also called Prakriti nature of Rajya or natural constituents of state. In literal, the word 'Saptanga' means seven limbs. This theory of Chanakya also gets its essence ancient Greek political philosophy. Chanakya states that they are like bodily Organs, eyes, ears, nose, hand etc. And if any one organ stops functioning the person will become impair. [1]Same goes for state machine all Organs needs to be in the working condition if some error occurs it may lead to breakdown of the state system.

Kautilya's particularized seven elements of state are:

I. Swami [ruler]

In the importance amongst the seven elements he gives highest importance to 'Swami'. Here by swami he refers to the monarch of the definite territory. He states it as the highest place in the body- politic. The meaning of the word 'swami' is 'swayam' which refers to self- determining. A swami has various protective and promotive functions. He should be born on the same soil he is ruling, should be from a noble family, well learned and had extensive powers.

In the scenario of contemporary Indian structure, the pure definition of swami cannot be justified as the rule of period and form of governance has a major change (monarchy to representative democracy). Here though the president is said to be the first citizen of the state, but many of the extensive powers rests with prime minister and does the field work of decision taking. Moreover, in the state with representative democracy as such India, the qualification of president and prime minister are at the distinguishable characteristic.

I. Amatya [ministers]

Amatya or mantrin represented the eyes of the state, according to Chanakya. He explains the recruitment of amatyas from higher order to lower. [2]Natural born citizens, honesty in financial matters, noble origin, energetic, qualities of bravery and long sight of the circumstances in any given situations are some of the categories. He did not mention a fixed number of amatyas to be recruited as it depended on the area of the territory. [3]

In today's scenario, India does have a ministry for various categories as an advisory to the prime minister and more precisely cabinet ministers. But the recruitment conditions differ from that of the Kautilyan period.

III. Janapada [The people and the territory]

The word Janapada denotes where people reside. Janapada represents the legs of the legs of the state. According to Kautilya a Janapada not just includes territory but also the residing population. This element lays down the general duties the 'Janas' have to follow, bonding their trust and respect to the swami and the territory. He included it as a element as it states to support and protect king.

The constitution of Indian state mentions or rather allots the fundamental duties which are to be respected by each citizen of the land.

IV. Durga [fortification of capital]

As the capital represents heart, he saw fortification of capital as an essential element as it provided security. It was given more importance than the other small regions within the territory.

All parts of Indian Territory are considered to be equally sovereign, infact some parts are more geo-strategically vital, large in area and abundant in resources.

V. Kosha [treasury]

He considers finance to be blood because of which the state runs. According to him it can be increased by taxation and plundering of enemy territories at war.

Treasury in Indian state mainly focuses on trade and taxation.

VI. Danda [coercive power of state]

Kautilya saw Danda as a very important aspect for a well control state. The Sena of a territory is considered to be the brain. The soldiers should not have close relations with relatives or family but only towards the state. He gave a complete different theory, elaborating more on Danda in his theory of Dandaniti.

The law and forces of modern India works on different principles yet the only aspect that's not changed is their dedication towards the land they are serving to. India's capability of covert actions which Kautilya refers to as 'silent war' is unknown especially in terms of accomplishments.

VII. Mitra [ally or friend]

Here in the context to the Kautilyan period it indicates friends of king or territories [4]whose swami is friend of king. It represents ears of the state.

In contemporary India it refers to the Indian foreign policy. But does not limit just to the friends from different countries as preferred by president and prime minister. Instead it has extended by morally signing of treating and becoming a member of varied international organization.

Though some of the elementary concepts of the Kautilyan period and contemporary period is similar, the application and practice of the same varies a lot throughout the time. The viewpoint of governance, state and politics has changed over the years and so is the applicability and pertinence of the elements of the state and thus is accordingly adapted with relevance to the dynamic society.

[1]Dr. TyagiRuchi, Theory of State in Kautilya'sArthashastra,

[2]Kangle, R.P.,KautilyaArthashastra, Pt III, Delhi, 1965

[3]KaurKiranjit ,Kautilya: Saptanga Theory Of State, The Indian Journal of Political Science, Vol. 71, No. 1, 2010

https://www.jstor.org/stable/42748368

[4] Dr. TyagiRuchi, Theory of State in Kautilya'sArthashastra

CHAPTER SIX

CONCLUSION

State being depicted as the center of society is regarded as a social organization that nurtures the social nature and ideals of the people. It is an elemental ground for the expansion of social duties of the people. Though the idea of Kautilya is relevant in the contemporary concept of state to a certain degree, the assertion of the same is quite different. The depiction and conception of sovereignty has changed over the period. Kautilya's philosophy is still a role model even in the present-day India but the applicability differs alongside the modern society. One cannot completely criticize or repulse the ideas of Chanakya as it is one of the leading factors for adaption of new policies and regulations for the contemporary state. The aspects and the factors essential for the state and its functioning have to be adapted in relevance to the contemporary times by referring to the illustrations provided by the progenitors.

Authors Bio

1] Kashish Darak

Pursuing BA LLB at Alliance University Bangalore. Born in Kolhapur, Maharashtra i have always been a confident and optimistic person. Human existence has always had the presence of law since history, its how it evolves and adapts to society.I find law fascinating in itself as I see it as regulatory of the society we live in.Taking law as a career I aim at becoming a judge and serving Indian state law.

2] Vaishnavi N

I am currently pursuing law at Alliance School of Law, Bengaluru. Being a CA aspirant, alongside accounting, law is the subject that interested me the most. Pursuing law is not only challenging but also interesting because of the involvement of research works. Being interested in pursuing corporate law, I aspire to be a legal advisor.

3] Aastha Sinha

Currently pursuing BA LLB (Hons) from Alliance university in Bangalore. Born and brought up in Patna.As an optimistic person I see myself being stable in my career, aiming to pursue in the field of corporate law.